Golfing Wit

summersdale

GOLFING WIT

Copyright © Summersdale Publishers Ltd, 2007
This selection was compiled by Aubrey Malone.
Illustrations by Ian Baker.
All rights reserved.

Reprinted 2008

Summersdale Publishers Ltd
46 West Street
Chichester
West Sussex
PO19 1RP
UK

www.summersdale.com

Printed and bound in Great Britain

ISBN 13: 978-1-84024-621-6

Golfing Wit

Aubrey Malone

Contents

Editor's Note

I'm not really gloating at the lovable losers or dotty eccentrics in this volume. They're more like my soulmates in crime, viewed from the relative safety of the 19th (hic!) hole. That's where you can sit over your pint and reminisce quietly about your purgatorial double bogeys as if they were perpetrated by someone else, and fantasise about the dream holes-in-one to a barman who probably won't care if they happened or not.

You can keep to yourself the manifold times you beheaded the ball, or hit your face with the club on your backswing as the divot went higher than a house and you found yourself begging for your fifth mulligan... on the same hole.

When I started this project I wasn't at all sure that the pros could be as (unintentionally) funny as yours truly. Nick Faldo? Bernhard Langer? Pul-eease! Better quote Phil Silvers' line: 'Be funny on a golf course? Do I kid my best friend's mother about her heart condition?'

But yes, dear reader, there was humour to be found, though not always where expected. I could have filled the book on Lee Trevino's expostulations alone but there were other unlikely jokesmiths too. Many of the jokes were rueful, and/or black, as one might be entitled to expect from a game that looks like heaven and feels like hell.

Some people call it terminally boring and others an unconquerable addiction. Somewhere in the middle of this fairway are the Walking (and Joking) Wounded. This is their story.

WHAT IS GOLF?

Golf is somewhere
between making love
and writing a poem.

John Updike

Golf is the loneliest of all games, not excluding postal chess.

Peter Dobereiner

Mark Twain said golf was a good walk spoiled. From which we can only conclude he'd either had a bad day on the course or, more likely, never played the game. A walk is a missed opportunity for golf.

Andrew Greig

Golf is a game that needlessly prolongs the lives of some of our most useless citizens.

Bob Hope

Golf is a game where
white men can dress
up as black pimps
and get away with it.

Robin Williams

Golf is like a love affair: if you don't take it seriously it's boring, and if you do it breaks your heart.

Rod Funseth

Golf is an 'umbling game.

Bobby Jones

Golf's not that hard. The ball doesn't move.

Ted Williams

Golf is not a funeral, though both can by very sad affairs.

Bernard Darwin

Golf was never meant to be an exact science. Einstein was lousy at it.

Bob Toski

Golf is a whore you go home to every day because a perverse part of your brain enjoys being tortured by her.

Anon

Golf is a game where you sock the ball hard and walk four feet.

Herbert Prochnow

The game was invented
for simpletons.

Spike Milligan

WHAT IS GOLF?

Golf should be played on Sunday, not being a game in the view of the law, but rather a form of moral effort.

Stephen Leacock

In Africa the natives have the custom of beating their clubs and uttering blood-curdling yells. Anthropologists call this a form of self-expression. In Europe we call it golf.

Phil Silver

Golf is a game in which players lie about their scores to people who used to be their friends after a day spent thrashing about on surfaces that look like spoiled pastures. That's why we take it up 'for the good of our health'.

Karen Durasch

WHERE IT ALL BEGAN

I sometimes wonder
how my mother
survived my childhood.

Jack Nicklaus

The best year of my life was when
I was 11. I won 32 tournaments
that year. Everything's
been downhill since.

Tiger Woods

When I first started golf, my
father told me I was going to
do more good than Gandhi,
Mother Teresa, the Pope and
Tony Blair all rolled into one.

Tiger Woods

Dad, what do people do on
Sunday who don't play golf?

Bobby Jones to his father as a child

My dentist recently discovered there was a narrow line of enamel missing from around my upper teeth. 'Did you suffer from malnutrition or a terrible disease as a child?' he asked. 'No,' I replied, 'just my mother's cooking.'

Nick Faldo

You shoulda seen it, Mom. Dad got to hit the ball more than anybody.

Dennis the Menace

I'll never play golf. It's a cissy game.

Arnold Palmer to his father at 15

If you made my life into a movie they'd say it was too far-fetched. In 1961 I left home with one suitcase, £5 in my pocket and a hand-me-down suit. A few years later Frank Sinatra was asking me if I wanted to fly back from Europe with him on his private jet.

Tony Jacklin

HIT AND MRS

Although we are told nothing about it, there can be little doubt that one of Job's chief trials was that his wife insisted on playing golf with him.

P. G. Wodehouse

Never insist that your spouse
golfs. It can lead to only two results.
One, she/he plays really badly,
complains for four hours and ruins
your whole day. Or, two, she/he
plays really well, offers four hours
of suggestions on how you might do
better, and ruins your whole day.

Ernie Witham

Husband: I got a new set
of clubs for my wife.
Friend: That sounds like a fair swap.

Bill Wannan

My wife and I are doing everything
we can to keep our marriage
together. We have candle-lit
dinners twice a week. She goes
Tuesdays, I go Fridays.

Walter Hagen

'Mildred, shut up,' cried the golfer at his nagging wife, 'shut up or you'll drive me out of my mind.' 'That,' snapped Mildred, 'wouldn't be a drive. That would be a putt.'

Deborah Kayser

***

I plan to be a golf widow next week. I've just bought the gun.

Joan Rivers

***

Golf wives are more 'Stepford' than 'Footballers'.

Robert O'Byrne

They say passion
for golf is a recipe for
mental illness. Logically
speaking, playing
with your wife should
double that danger.

Les Dawson

When I come back in the next
life I want to be a golf pro's wife.
She wakes up every morning at
the crack of ten and is faced with
her first major decision of the day:
whether to have breakfast in bed
or in the hotel coffee shop.

Dan Sikes

All my exes wear Rolexes.

John Daly

Golf is wrecking my head.
Yesterday I kissed my seven-iron
goodbye and putted my wife.

Don Rickles

Footballers' wives fall out of taxis
blathered at 3 a.m. in red-light
districts. The worst a golf wife does
is wear an uncoordinated dress.

Shelly Kirkland

That's what happens when you
haven't been home in 18 years.

Lee Trevino on his divorce

Give me my golf clubs, fresh air and
a beautiful partner and you can keep
the golf clubs and the fresh air.

Jack Benny

Our relationship lasted longer
than either of his two marriages.

Nick Faldo's coach David Leadbetter, who
was sacked by Faldo after 13 years

Playing with your spouse on the
golf course runs almost as great a
marital risk as getting caught playing
with someone else's anywhere else.

Peter Andrews

A fanatical golfer is speaking to
his friend. 'For years I didn't know
where my wife spent her evenings,'
he says. The friend asks him how he
finally found out. 'Well, one evening
I went home and there she was.'

George Burns

Golf and sex are the only two things you can enjoy without being good at either of them.

Jim Davidson

———

'After all, golf is only a game,' said Millicent. Women say these things without thinking. It does not mean that there is any kink in their character. They simply don't realise what they are saying.

P. G. Wodehouse

———

My wife: You and Jim have played golf every Sunday for years. Wouldn't you like to invite him and his wife to dinner?
Me: Jim is married?

David Owen

Ladies: If he comes home from the golf course looking like he's been at the beach, it's not a good time to ask him about that new dress.

Fran Lebowitz

My wife doesn't care what I do when I'm away as long as I don't have fun.

Lee Trevino

THE CRUEL GAME

Every time I feel the urge to play golf I go into a corner and put a wet towel over my head until it passes.

Sam Levenson

Give me a man with big hands,
big feet and no brains and I will
make a golfer out of him.

Walter Hagen

———•———

I thought about taking up golf...
and then I thought again.

Groucho Marx

———•———

The most maddening thing about
golf is the perversity with which the
body refuses to obey the mind.

Pat Ward-Thomas

Everyone gets wounded in a game
of golf. The trick is not to bleed.

Peter Dobereiner

I've been playing golf for 20
years now and have just made
a discovery. I hate it.

Rex Beach

Golf has given me an understanding
of the futility of life.

Aubrey Eban

I've never been depressed
enough to take up the game.

Will Rogers

I don't want to play golf.
When I hit a ball, I expect
someone else to run after it.

Jackie Gleason

I heard some good news today. Ten
golfers a year are hit by lightning.

George Carlin

O. J. Simpson has already
received the ultimate punishment.
For the rest of his life he has
to associate with golfers.

George Carlin

What is needed instead of all
these instructional books on how
to play golf is a walloping good
book on how to give it up.

Michael Green

Golf is the cruellest of sports. It's
a harlot, an obsession, a boulevard
of broken dreams. It plays with men
and runs off with the butcher.

Jim Murray

Any time you feel
the urge to golf,
instead take 18
minutes and beat
your head against
a good solid wall.
This is guaranteed
to duplicate to a
tee the physical and
emotional beating you
would have suffered
playing a round.

Mark Oman

SLOWCOACHES

There was a thunderous
crack like cannonfire
and suddenly I was
lifted a foot and a half
off the ground. There
was a loud ringing in
my ears like a tuning
fork, my hands were
flailing and I couldn't
breathe. I was stretched
out like a vibrator.
Damn, I thought to
myself, this is a helluva
penalty for slow play.

Lee Trevino on being struck by lightning

Golf teaches us that although patience is a virtue, slow play is not.

Marc Gellman

———•———

The marshall pointed out that we were holding up play so badly, the golfers behind us were building shelters for the night, and the management had set up soup kitchens and group counselling.

Michael Parkinson

———•———

Golf is a game in which the slowest people in the world are in front of you, and the fastest ones behind.

Kevin McCarthy

Ken Brown doesn't need a watch to time himself on a golf course. He needs a calendar.

Bud Eglinton

The best way to deal with people hassling you to play faster is to let them through – and then hassle *them*.

Jack Benny

'What's he waiting for?' said the spectator as he watched a player stand motionless over his ball. His friend replied, 'He's waiting for the grass to grow up under it and give him a better lie.'

Bobby Jones

EXERCISING ONE'S PREROGATIVE

Golf gives you about as much exercise as shuffling cards.

Bill Cosby

It looks like a very good exercise,
but what's the little white ball for?

Ulysses S. Grant upon seeing his first game of golf

At my age I try to work out a
little. I go swimming twice a day.
It beats buying golf balls.

Bob Hope

The greatest liar in the world is
the golfer who claims he plays
the game merely for exercise.

Tommy Bolt

Arnold Palmer has gone on a fitness programme. He's given up cigarettes and started jogging. He only coughs now when his opponent is putting.

Bing Crosby

Playing a sport and breathing air in spite of an increasing girth, poor eyesight, a dicky heart, varicose veins and high blood pressure is a defiant gesture by those whose lives are otherwise devoted to concentrated dissipation and indulgence.

Peter Gammond

Golf teaches us that even people who wear green pants deserve some place where they can go, get a little exercise, and not be laughed at.

Marc Gellman

THE 19TH HOLE

The 19th hole is
the only one where
players can have
as many shots
as they like.

Louis Safian

What scoundrel took the
cork out of my lunch?

W. C. Fields during a 'snack' break
at the Lakeside Club in LA

A policeman pulled me over
when I had one too many.
'Are you intending to drive
home, sir?' he asked. 'Well, you
don't expect me to walk in this
condition, do you?' I replied.

Doug Sanders, attrib.

Arsenic.

Ben Crenshaw to a bartender who asked
him what he wanted to drink after he failed
to qualify for the British Open in 1992

My favourite hole was
always the watering hole.

Ronan Rafferty

❧

The first time I played the Masters
I was so nervous I drank a bottle
of rum before I teed off. I shot
the happiest 83 of my life.

Chi Chi Rodriguez

❧

I'll drink to that.

Jimmy Demaret after a colleague told him he'd win
more tournaments if he eased off on the bottle

Scotland is the birthplace of golf and salmon fishing. Which may explain why it is also the birthplace of whisky.

Henry Beard

My players sank the white and now I'm going to sink the black.

Ian Woosnam promising to lower some Guinness after his team won the Ryder Cup in Ireland in 2006

In Ireland the 19th hole is mandatory, as are 20 and 21.

Bill Murray

W. C. Fields carried a hip flask of whisky in his back pocket when he golfed. One day after imbibing a glass too many he keeled over on the 18th tee. A crew of minders rushed over to him as he writhed in agony.

'Are you all right?' one of them enquired. Fields looked at the liquid running down his leg and smiled. 'Thank God it's only blood,' he said.

Don Rickles

The 19th is the most important hole
of all . When you get there you have
to work on your stance and also keep
your eyes focussed downwards. Make
sure there's dead silence around you
as you grip the glass with both hands,
the left thumb slightly protruding.
Avoid twisting your elbow too much
on the downward spiral. Ease it gently
back onto the counter before releasing
your grip, then order another one.

Jeffrey Bernard

I once called his hotel room the
morning after a convivial meeting.
I said, 'Is that Lee Trevino?' A
bleary voice answered, 'Wait a
minute. Let me look in the mirror.'

Gary Player

The bartender in the clubhouse hears so many stories about missed opportunities and failed lives, he could charge analysis fees. He shouldn't put out bar-stools. Couches would be more appropriate.

Robert Powell

Somebody said once that every Irishman wanted to buy Christy O'Connor a drink – and that most had succeeded.

Christy O'Connor

If you drink, don't drive. Don't even putt.

Dean Martin

If you go to Ireland with a
small hangover you'll come
home with a big one.

Sam Torrance

⬥

Doug Sanders only drinks
socially now. He keeps a bottle
of Socially in the clubhouse.

John Forsythe

⬥

'Greenkeeper, I dropped my bottle
of Scotch out of the bag somewhere
on the seventh. Anything handed
in at lost-and-found?' 'Only the
golfer who played after you, sir.'

Robert McCune

CLOTHES LINES

There's too much fussiness in golf clubs. I was asked to leave my last one because my socks weren't colour coordinated with my umbrella.

Mildred Sassoon

They didn't wear Plus Fours
because they were crack players.
They were crack players because
they wore Plus Fours.

P. G. Wodehouse

I had to change into brown
trousers after playing my
first hole at the Masters.

Trevor Homer

I hope you're wearing that for a bet.

Colin Montgomerie to Payne Stewart

The golfing girl of today should
indeed be grateful that she need
not play in a sailor hat, a high
stiff collar, a voluminous skirt
and petticoats, a motor veil or a
wide skirt with leather binding.

Mabel Stringer

I have known girls to become golfers
as an excuse to wear pink jumpers.

P. G. Wodehouse

Among Jimmy Demaret's outfits was
a 'golf tuxedo', made without armpit
seams to allow for a free swing.

Geoff Tibballs

My gaad, I've got socks
older than you.

Lee Trevino to a 27-year-old opponent
at a tournament in 1980

Jackie Gleason once donated
a sweater to a charity as a
pro-am prize. Now there's a
family of refugees living in it.

Bob Hope

The older I get, the less
inclined I am to dress for golf
as if for a polar expedition.

Michael Parkinson

Palm Springs is a great golf town.
They won't let you in unless you're
wearing an alpaca sweater.

Bob Hope

Although golf was originally
restricted to wealthy, overweight
Protestants, today it's open to
anybody who owns hideous clothing.

Dave Barry

Azinger is wearing an all black outfit:
black jumper, blue trousers, white
shoes and a pink tea cosy hat.

Renton Laidlaw

'Play it as it lies' is one of the
fundamental dictates of golf. The
other is, 'Wear it if it clashes'.

Henry Beard

I wish they'd start talking about the quality of my golf, not my wardrobe. Print my score, not my measurements.

Craig Stadler

It appears that Canadian golfers are more laid-back than us Scots about clothing. A club in British Columbia has a sign which warns, 'No spikes on dance floor'.

Tom Shields

Golf is not a sport. Golf is men in ugly pants, walking.

Rosie O'Donnell

Doug Sanders' outfit has
been described as looking
like the aftermath of a direct
hit on a pizza factory.

Dave Marr

George Burns looked perfect
in his alpaca sweater, his knitted
shirt and the best woods money
could buy. What a pity he had
to ruin it all by playing golf.

Lloyd Mangrum

I'd give up golf if I didn't
have so many sweaters.

Bob Hope

'Officer, I've just been knocked
down by my friend in a golf cart.'
'What gear was he in?'
'The usual woolly jumper
and Nike runners.'

Liam O'Mahony

I don't like playing in Scotland;
I can't swing the way I want to
wearing four sweaters, a rain
jacket, and my pyjamas.

Lee Trevino

HOT SHOTS

It must have been the greatest four-wood anyone ever hit. It was so much on the flag I had to lean sideways to follow the flight of the ball.

Gary Player

The hardest shot is the 90-yard chip from the green where the ball has to be played against an oak, bounces back into a sandtrap, hits a stone, bounces onto the green and then rolls into the cup. It's so difficult I've only made it once.

Zeppo Marx

There are days when you feel you can't miss even when you try to.

Jack Nicklaus

Golf shots aren't bullets, they're arrows.

Greg Norman

It was so good I could nearly feel the baby applauding.

A seven-months-pregnant Donna White after a good putt

My driving is so good these
days I have to dial the operator
long distance after I hit it.

Lee Trevino

I always had the feeling that the
ground shook when Nick Faldo
made contact with the ball.

Dave Cannon

Colin Montgomerie hit a three-
wood 300 yards down the left side
of the fairway. If he'd rented a car,
filled the tank full of rocket fuel
and brought along an Ordnance
Survey map of the West Midlands
he couldn't have sent it any further.

Lawrence Donegan

All of us believe that our good
shots are the norm, and our
bad ones aberrations.

Alec Morrison

When you hit a good shot and your
playing partner says, 'Great shot!'
you're supposed to murmur, 'Oh,
I don't know', or 'Lucky bounce',
while inside every fibre silently
exults, 'That was frickin' fabulous'.

Andrew Greig

A straight drive or a short chip
stiff to the pin gives a player the
bliss that used to come thinking
of women, imagining if only he and
she were alone on some island.

John Updike

GOLF TIPS

Golf tips are like aspirin. One may do you good, but if you swallow the whole bottle you'll be lucky to survive.

Harvey Pennick

Never give up a hole. Quitting between tee and green is more habit-forming than drinking highballs before breakfast.

Sam Snead

To improve my golf, I once read one of those great involved books on positive thinking. I gave up when I heard the author committed suicide.

Nick Job

I tee the ball high because years of experience have shown me that air offers less resistance than dirt.

Jack Nicklaus

The secret of missing a tree
is to aim straight for it.

Michael Green

———•———

Never try to keep more than
300 separate thoughts in your
mind during your swing.

Henry Beard

———•———

Never break your putter and
your driver in the same round.

Tommy Bolt

In his younger days, Andy Bean
developed a taste for snacking on
golf balls and wrestling alligators.
He might have been better
advised to swap things around.

Geoff Tibballs

Drive for show, putt for dough.

Ernie Els

Drive for show, putt for dough,
shank for Comic Relief.

Sticker

If you're making a deal with a business associate on a golf course, make sure you fine-tune it before he tees off. Particularly if you've got a mortgage – or a heart condition.

Tom Smothers

The best time to take up golf is about ten years ago.

Leslie Nielsen

The secret of good golf is to play it as though it were a game.

Doug Gambon

Relax into a rhythm that fits the
hills and swales and play the shot
at hand – not the last one, not the
next one, but the one at your feet,
in the poison ivy, where you put it.

John Updike

Take time to smell the flowers
on your way round.

Walter Hagen

———◆———

I've been taking Walter Hagen's
advice and it's working a treat.
Every time I bend down I find
one of my lost balls in them.

Russ Abbot

———◆———

Don't ever make eye contact
with a golf name-dropper. Once
he locks on you you're liable to
get the full treatment: 'I just said
"Hi" to Tiger'. 'I've just seen
Monty taking a pee'. 'Padraig's
over there scratching his balls'.

Ross Robertson

Hit it a bloody sight harder!

Ted Ray after a novice asked him how he
might get the ball to travel further

—◆—

Never give another golfer
unsolicited advice, including the
advice to never give another
golfer unsolicited advice.

Leslie Nielsen

—◆—

Golf should never be played
on any day with a 'y' in it.

Les Dawson

PRACTICE MAKES PERFECT

I have taught golf at a driving-range for some time and have seen many people actually practising mistakes.

Mel Flanagan

I hate practice, my idea of warming
up is a double egg, sausage,
bacon and fried bread.

Michael Parkinson

Golf teaches us that although
practice doesn't always make perfect,
no practice always makes us imperfect.

Tom Hartman

I don't practise much these days.
At my age, you need to keep all
your energy for your actual shots.

Sam Snead at 78

The novice had a problem. He was able to make a perfect practice swing, but when the ball went down it all seemed to disintegrate. He explained to the pro, 'How is it that every time I line up to hit a daisy I have no problem? I'm able to clip the head off it, but when the ball goes down I miss it completely.' The pro thought for a moment before advising, 'Why don't you put the ball on top of the daisy?'

Mel Flanagan

They call me a natural player.
So why do I have to practise
till my hands bleed?

Seve Ballesteros

❧

Swinging at daisies is a bit like
playing the electric guitar with a
tennis racquet. If it were that easy
we could all be Jerry Garcia.
The ball changes everything.

Michael Bamberger

❧

All I know is I've seen Nicklaus watch
Hogan practise, but I've never seen
Hogan watch Nicklaus practise.

Tommy Bolt to Christy O'Connor after being
asked to compare the two golfers

And then there was the condemned
golfer who asked the hangman,
'Mind if I take a few practice swings?'

Hal Roach

❦

I remember watching Gary Player
practising pitching on to a downhill
slope, the ground like concrete, trying
to get the ball to stop within 25 feet.
In the nicest possible way I suggested
he return to South Africa, enjoy
golf as an amateur and get a steady
job that might include a pension.

Peter Alliss

❦

When Julius Boros putts, you
can't tell by looking whether
he's just practising or it's
fifty grand if he sinks it.

Lee Trevino

For practice, Johnny McDermott used to hit balls onto a newspaper in a field. The story goes that he got mad if his ball failed to land on the right paragraph.

Charles Price

I've been practising my swing in front
of the mirror for a few months and it's
working a treat. I'm now thoroughly
proficient at hitting... mirrors.

John Denver

LET'S PUTT IT
LIKE THIS

Putting allows the
touchy golfer two to
four opportunities
to blow a gasket in
the short space of
two to 40 feet.

Tommy Bolt

Non-golfers have unrealistic ideas about the difficulty of putting. Powder a long drive deep into the woods and they'll ooh and aah, but miss from six feet and they'll look at you as though you should be in a padded cell.

Jack Nicklaus

Whoever said putting was a pleasure obviously never played golf.

Michael Green

There are three things a man must do alone: testify, die, and putt.

Bennett Cerf

I was putting like a
lobotomised baboon.

Tony Johnston

The only time Clayton Heafner
could putt was when he got mad
enough to hate the ball into the hole.

Cary Middlecoff

The devoted golfer is an anguished
soul who has learned a lot about
putting, just as an avalanche victim
has learned a lot about snow.

Dan Jenkins

The Coarse Golfer: one who has to shout 'Fore' when he putts.

Michael Green

———

Putt in haste and repent at leisure.

Gerald Batchelor

———

A putt that's struck too hard has only one way into the cup – through the middle of the front door. There's no tradesman's entrance.

Bobby Jones

I think I know the answer to your putting problems. You need to hit the ball closer to the hole.

Valerie Hogan to her legendary husband Ben

WEIGHT WATCHERS

Golf and cricket
are the only two
games where you can
actually put on weight
while playing them.

Tommy Docherty

Some guys try to shoot
their age. Craig Stadler
tries to shoot his weight.

Jim Murray

The best way to lose weight
at golf is to go to a Mexican
course and drink the water.

Buddy Hackett

Corey Pavin looks like he was
in a famine. Craig Stadler
looks like he caused it.

Andy Williams

Most of the guys on the tour are built like truck drivers but have the touch of hairdressers. Charlie Price is built like a hairdresser and he has the touch of a truck driver.

Clayton Heafner

It takes a lot of guts to play golf, and if you look at Billy Caspar you can tell he has a lot of guts.

Gary Player

I've lost 40 pounds since Christmas – 150 if you include the wife.

David Feherty after his divorce

The fat bellies
have slimmed down
as the purses have
grown fatter.

Sam Torrance

ER, COME AGAIN?

My 15 minutes
of fame ran to
almost a decade.

Laura Baugh

Tenison was the hardest
easy course I ever played.

Lee Trevino

❈

Seve Ballesteros is relaxed
in an intense sort of way.

Colin Montgomerie

❈

I would like to thank the press
from the heart of my bottom.

Nick Faldo after winning the Open in 1992

Ballesteros felt much
better today after a 69.

Steve Ryder commenting on the US Masters

95 per cent of putts which
finish short don't go in.

Robert Green

Pinero has missed the putt. I wonder
what he's thinking in Spanish.

Renton Laidlaw

I'm learning not to
get too excited after
one good round and
to keep my head
on the ground.

Colin Montgomerie

Nick Faldo this afternoon is
all in blue, with a white shirt.

Tony Adamson

I would like to thank my parents
– especially my father and mother.

Greg Norman during his winning speech at
the 1993 World Matchplay Championship

I think I can just see the
corner of the ball.

Jack Newton

I must play less in order to prolong my career.

Seve Ballesteros

I'm yesterday's man, or rather I will be tomorrow.

Peter McEvoy

This is Vincente Fernandez of Argentina. You will notice that he walks with a slight limp. This is because he was born with one leg shorter than the other two.

Roddy Carr while commenting on the Irish Open

It would have been a birdie
if the ball hadn't stopped
before it reached the hole.

David Coleman

If golf wasn't my living I wouldn't
play it if you paid me.

Christy O'Connor

Hindsight is always 50/50.

Charlie Drake

So, Woosie, you're from Wales.
What part of Scotland is that?

American journalist to Ian Woosnam
during a 1987 press conference

Gary Player had to be a better
golfer than Jack Nicklaus
in order to be as good.

Peter Dobereiner

THE FEMALE OF
THE SPECIES

If it wasn't for golf, I'd
probably be the fat
lady in the circus now.

Kathy Whitworth

My driving style? I just loosen my girdle and let her rip.

Babe Zaharias

I achieved a lot by climbing over
113 golfers. The only problem was
that there were 114 ahead of me.

Joanne Carner after securing the runners-
up spot in the U.S. Women's Open, having
recovered from 115th place after the first round

If a woman can walk,
she can play golf.

Louise Suggs

I'd like to see Bo Derek
after 18 holes in 100-degree
weather. Those cornrows and
beads would be history.

Jan Stephenson

I'll take a two-shot penalty, but
I'll be damned if I'm going to
play the ball where it lies.

Elaine Johnson in 1982 after her tee-shot
rebounded off a tree and ended up in her bra

HOLES-IN-ONE

In Japan you can take
out insurance against
hitting a hole-in-one
because by tradition
you then have to host a
party for the golf club
members and shower
your golfing partners,
your caddy and all your
friends with expensive
gifts, as well as planting
a commemorative
tree on the course.

Des Lynam

If your opponent in a money match gets a hole-in-one shortly after he tells you he hasn't played the game in months, count your fingers after he shakes hands with you.

Jackie Gleason

A hole-in-one is as much a rite of passage as hearing your first four-lettered word at a football match, singing Eskimo Nell on your first rugby tour, or finding out the meaning of life when hit on the box from a quick bowler.

Michael Parkinson

Harry Gonder once hit 1,817 shots at a hole over 16 hours and 25 minutes in an attempt to prove he could get a hole-in-one if he persevered. Failing in his ambition, he trudged back to the clubhouse certain that the law of averages was an ass.

David Randall

I don't believe in George Bush, the tooth fairy, and guys who get holes-in-one when nobody is looking.

Rich Hall

Always tell the truth. You may make a hole-in-one when you're alone on the golf course some day.

Franklin P. Jones

The highlight of the tournament
came when Arnold Palmer scored
a hole-in-one. A deafening roar
went up. A steward asked me
what all the noise was for and I
told him what Arnold had done.
'Well, so he should,' he replied.
'He plays often enough.'

Jimmy Tarbuck

———◆———

A distinguished Professor of
Pathology, who recently holed
out in one at the 4th at Walton
Heath, thus opening the round
with a 4371444, asked whether
he was the only man in history
to have started a round with
his own telephone number.

Harry Longhurst

It's a pity I don't have a video of the hole-in-one I once made, but they weren't invented then.

Bob Monkhouse

Did you hear about the golfer who killed the Puerto Rican? He shot a hole in Juan.

Chubby Brown

The reason golfers wear two pairs of socks is because they're hoping they'll get a hole in one.

Ronan Keating

The club grouch was unhappy about everything: the food, the assessments, the parking, the other members. The first time he hit a hole-in-one he complained. 'Damn it – just when I needed the putting practice!'

Joey Adams

PREFERRED LIES

In golf the ball
usually lies poorly,
and the player well.

William Davies

Truth is something you leave in
the locker room with your street
shoes when you play golf.

Terry Martin

Nothing handicaps you so
much in golf as honesty.

Oliver Cronin

A lie is either where the ball
has come to rest or where the
player claims it came to rest.

Peter Gammond

Golfers start by excusing poor shots by claiming bad lies. With time, such lies improve dramatically.

Chevy Chase

Question on golf etiquette: What do you do when your opponent claims to have found his ball in the rough, and you know he's a liar because you've got it in your pocket?

George Coote

A tough lie is when you have to come up with an excuse as to why it took six hours to play nine holes and why your breath smells like nacho chips and beer.

Ernie Witham

The one reward golf has given me, and I shall always be thankful for it, is introducing me to some of the world's most picturesque, tireless and bald-faced liars.

Ring Lardner

MAGNIFICENT OBSESSION

Real golfers go to
work to relax.

George Dillon

My wife says if I don't give
up golf she'll leave me.
That's terrible.
I know. I'm really going to miss her.

Exchange between Eric Morecambe and Ernie Wise

❧

I'll play golf until I die, and then
I want them to roll me into a
bunker, cover me with sand
and make sure nobody's ball
lands in there for a while.

Lee Trevino

❧

Golf is my profession.
Show business is just to
pay the green fees.

Bob Hope

Golf is not a relaxation.
Golf is a religion.

Sir Bob Reid

The long par five 9th hole
at Llanymynech has a huge
significance for me. There was a
15-yard hollow stretching across
the fairway. School work, the moon
landings, England's painful 3–2
defeat against West Germany in
the 1970 World Cup – nothing
mattered as much to me as hitting
my drive past that hollow.

Ian Woosnam

Andrew came rushing into the clubhouse in a state of great agitation. 'I've just sliced the ball into a tree,' he said, 'but it rebounded and went onto the road where it hit the rider of a motorbike who fell off his bike. Then a lorry ran into him, causing its load of onions to spill all over the road, which has caused more cars to crash, so there are bodies and smashed vehicles all over the place. What can I do?' The club president thought deeply for a moment and then suggested, 'Take it a bit easier on the backswing in future.'

Kevin Goldstein-Jackson

There are only two types of people
in the world: golfers and non-golfers.
Once bitten, it is akin to having your
neck punctured in Transylvania
– there is no known antidote.

Martin Johnson

The reason golf obsesses
so many is that it answers a
latent lunacy in its devotees, or
perhaps by its frustrations and
impossibilities tips them into one.

A. C. Grayling

Golfers are a level-headed lot. They
only talk about golf three times a
day: before they play, while they're
playing, and after they've played.

Katharine Whitehorn

I have it on good authority that the manager of one of Ireland's best rock 'n' roll bands, given the choice of the lads being addicted to heroin or golf, said he would marginally prefer if they took to the heroin. 'If they're on smack, you can at least kick them into a taxi and throw them onto a plane, but if they're out golfing you can't even find the bastards.'

Declan Lynch

What is love compared to holing out before your opponent?

P. G. Wodehouse

You know you're a bit weird when you ask for *Golf Digest* bedtime stories at three.

John Ellis

CONUNDRUMS

How is it that a man can push a lawnmower for an hour and call it work, but when he pushes a golf cart all day he calls it recreation?

Leopold Fechtner

Why is it called a three-wood
when it's made out of metal?

Ernie Witham

❦

If the universe is finite, as people
say, how come golfers never
find all the balls they lose?

Hal Roach

❦

Do golfers' drives put them crazy
or their putts drive them crazy?

Valerie Ferguson

Is it any accident that 'God' comes just before 'golf' in the dictionary?

Dave Allen

If golf is a rich man's game, how come there are so many poor players?

Mitch Murray

The true secret of golf is: One day you play really well and the next really crap – and you don't know why.

Patrick Rayner

THE UNKINDEST CUTS OF ALL

The rising hum of suburban hysteria for this event is the overture for Ireland's slide towards a suffocating blandness. It has nothing indigenous to ourselves. It's just a tasteless mush of middle-class objectives.

Michael Moynihan on the 2006 Ryder Cup

When Paul Azinger turned professional in 1981 it was as though the village idiot had just announced his intention to pursue a career in astrophysics.

Bill Elliot

❧

Deane Beman couldn't hit the ball out of his own shadow.

Peter Alliss

❧

You don't have to keep score when you play golf with Jerry Ford. You just look back along the fairway and follow the wounded.

Bob Hope

His judgment of line and length were such that a blindfold would only have improved matters.

Michael Parkinson on a hapless colleague

A nice old lady with a croquet mallet could have saved him two strokes.

Bernard Darwin on Bobby Jones' pitiful display at the British Open in 1930

Pool player to caddy: I'm not playing the game I used to. Caddy: What game was that?

Steve Porrest

Anything that moves
– and everything
that's nailed down
– has a sponsor.

Miriam Lord on the Ryder Cup

Like Joseph Conrad, Greg Norman began life as a seaman, although there the similarity ends. Conrad would not have crouched down over a sprinkler-head to examine his putt at the very moment the gamekeeper switched on the irrigation. He would not have turned up at the Italian Open with no trousers. He definitely wouldn't have fallen off his chair during a live radio report and carried on discussing the leaders while lying on his back amid the wreckage.

Lauren St John

What's the difference between Gordon Bland and a coconut? You can get a drink out of a coconut.

Simon Hobday

What do Tiger Woods and his blonde fiancée have in common? They both have black roots.

Anon

———◆———

There are 56 million golfers in the world. Which only goes to show you what a silly place the world is.

Kenny Lynch

———◆———

When we arrive you can see the secretary flicking through the book and thinking, 'Why have these guys turned up? No one ordered a taxi or a takeaway'.

Asian Open chairman Jaz Athwal on racism in golf

Colin Montgomerie walks round a golf course like a man under the impression that smiling gives you herpes.

Lawrence Donegan

Europe did their best to help America win the Ryder Cup in 2006. We picked Ian Woosnam as captain.

Oliver Holt

I wouldn't recommend golf to my worst enemy. Actually on second thoughts I would.

John Wayne

SELF-ABUSE

I have often been
gratefully aware of
the heroic efforts
of my opponents
not to laugh at me.

Bernard Darwin

My most notable trait is snatching defeat out of the jaws of victory.

Doug Saunders

I wouldn't know a nine-iron from a steam iron.

Lise Hand

I'm a solid player apart from a drink problem, the yips, and a tendency to break my clubs every time I hit a bad shot.

Simon Hobday

A: Why aren't you playing golf
with the colonel any more?
B: Would you play with a man who
swears and curses with every shot,
who cheats in the bunkers and who
enters false scores on his cards?
A: Certainly not!
B: Well, neither will the colonel.

Freddie Oliver

❦

I call golf 'Connect the sand traps'. I
can play four or five rounds without
having the ball touch grass once.

Jack Benny

❦

My game's gone off so much that
when I went fishing a couple of weeks
ago my first cast missed the lake.

Ben Crenshaw in 1977

SELF-ABUSE

I'm into golf now. I'm getting pretty
good. I can almost hit the ball as
far as I can throw the clubs.

Bob Ettinger

I don't rent golf carts. I don't
need them. Where I hit the ball, I
can use public transportation.

Gene Perret

Maybe I should go to a sports
shop and buy a trophy. That's the
only way I'm going to get one.

Seve Ballesteros during a bad spell in his career

Spell 'golf' backwards and
you have a pretty good idea
of my playing style.

George Burns

I played so badly I got a get-well
card from the Inland Revenue.

Johnny Miller in 1977

———◆———

I tried to play like Jack Nicklaus, but
ended up more like Jacques Tati.

David Feherty after a poor display in 1992

———◆———

It took me 17 years to get 3,000 hits
in baseball. I did the same thing in
one afternoon on the golf course.

Hank Aaron

———◆———

Golf.

**Jackie Gleason after being asked
what his handicap was**

We couldn't hit a cow's arse with a banjo.

Mark James on the Ryder Cup team in 1977

I play golf like Cinderella. I
never make it to the ball.

Don Rickles

———◆———

You learn a lot about yourself
by playing golf. Unfortunately,
most of it is unprintable.

Burt Lancaster

———◆———

The things I don't know about
golf would fill a very large book.

Leslie Nielsen, who actually went on to write one

———◆———

I can airmail the golf ball,
but sometimes I don't put
the right address on it.

Jim Dent

I was reading the other day that
there are 2,000 different ways
you can hit the ball wrong. So far
I think I've reached about 1,800.

Dinah Shore

My career started slowly,
then tapered off.

Gary McCord

If my IQ had been two points
lower I'd have been a plant.

Lee Trevino

HERE'S TO THE LOSERS

The only thing I ever
learned from losing
was that I don't like it.

Tom Watson

Few things draw two men
together more than a mutual
inability to play golf.

P. G. Wodehouse

Defeat is worse than death, because
you have to live with defeat.

Nick Faldo

I find it more satisfying to be a
bad player at golf. The worse you
play, the better you remember
the occasional good shot.

Nubar Gulbenkian

Golf is popular because it is the best game in the world at which to be bad. It is, after all, the bad player who gets the most strokes.

A. A. Milne

Golf is the only game where the worst player gets the best of it. He obtains more out of it as regards exercise and enjoyment, because the good player worries over the slightest mistake, whereas the poor one makes too many to worry about them.

David Lloyd George

I never liked team sports because it annoyed me that if you did your bit you could still go home a loser.

Nick Faldo

Show me a good loser and
I'll show you a loser.

Gary Player

———————

Show me a man who's a good
loser and I'll show you a man
who's playing golf with his boss.

Jim Murray

———————

There were a number of reasons
my golfing career was cut short:
lack of time, a disinclination to
practise... and the fact that I
was utterly and totally crap.

Michael O'Driscoll

CADDYSHACK

The first thing to
understand about
caddying is that it's
not brain surgery.
It's much more
complicated than that.

Lawrence Donegan

Players make mistakes.
Caddys make blunders.

Jerry Osborne

———•———

A campaign is afoot to bring the caddy back to American golf courses. In *Golf Digest* and elsewhere you can read of the many benefits. It's better for the ageing golfer's cardiovascular system to walk than to ride, better for the course not to have motorised cars flattening the grass into shiny highways of dying turf, better for the caddy himself to be lugging two 20-pound bags than flipping cholesterol-rich hamburgers at McDonald's.

John Updike

After his last shot, Mr Smith turned to his caddy and asked, 'What did you think of my game?' The caddy thought for a moment and then replied, 'Quite good, sir, but I prefer golf myself.'

Kevin Goldstein-Jackson

I once sank a 35-yard putt against Billy Graham. When I turned round I saw my caddy had been turned into a pillar of salt.

Bob Hope

Divorces between caddys and players are often executed on the spot, and there isn't any alimony.

John O'Reilly

Golfer to caddy after messing up a
shot: Golf is a funny old game, innit?
Caddy: The way you play
it it certainly is, sir.

Greg Doherty

———◆———

There's a man playing golf and
his caddy spends ages finding
him the right club. 'Oh, come on,
man,' he says, 'you must be the
worst caddy on earth.' 'I doubt
it,' the caddy replies, 'that would
be too much of a coincidence.'

Frank Muir

———◆———

A bunch of bums who whistle
through their teeth, don't know which
club to put into my hand, and smell
strongly of BO, alcohol, or both.

Sam Snead on the St Andrews caddys

I never kick my ball in the rough
or improve my lie in a sand trap.
For that I have a caddy.

Bob Hope

Real golfers, no matter what the
provocation, never strike a caddy
with the driver. The sand wedge
is infinitely more effective.

Huxtable Pippey

If each time a player and caddy
split up was actually a divorce,
most tour players would have been
married more times than Zsa Zsa
Gabor and Liz Taylor combined.

Peter Jacobsen

Andrew Whitacre is the perfect caddy. Scratch handicap, former psychology major, and no outstanding warrants.

Bill Murray

—◆—

There were three things in the world that he held in the smallest esteem: slugs, poets, and caddys with hiccups.

P. G. Wodehouse

—◆—

I asked my caddy if I had a shot to the green. He replied, 'Mr Murray, I would say you have several shots to the green.'

Ian Murray

I asked Marilyn Monroe if she'd come golfing with me one day. 'I can't,' she said, 'I don't even know how to hold the caddy.'

Dean Martin

After bumping four balls into the rough on the spin, I asked my caddy what I should take for my next shot. 'Either a cyanide capsule,' he replied, 'or the next plane home.'

Jack Lemmon

"YOUR LANDSCAPE GARDENING SKILLS ARE SECOND TO NONE MA'AM!"

And then there was the golfer
who said to her caddy, 'Notice
any improvement today, Jack?'
And Jack replies, 'Yes, ma'am,
I see you got your hair done.'

Stuart Whitley

ODIOUS COMPARISONS

Colin Montgomerie
has a face like a
warthog that's been
stung by a wasp.
David Feherty

Ballesteros goes after a golf course
the way a lion goes after a cobra.

Jim Murray

Golf is like love or the measles.
You're better off if you
get over it early in life.

G. K. Chesterton

My golfing career? On one hole
I'm like Arnold Palmer, and then
at the next I'm Lilli Palmer.

Sean Connery

Every time Padraig Harrington hits a great shot he looks like a wino who's just found a tenner in his inside pocket.

Lawrence Donegan

I once made an effort to master elephant polo in Delhi. It was a bit like playing golf with a fishing rod.

Max Boyce

In 1991 Tom Sieckman won the Philippine Open, the Thailand Open and the Singapore Open, leaving him second only to the US Marines for victories in the Pacific.

Gary Nuhm

Golf balls are attracted to water as unerringly as the eye of a middle-aged man to a female bosom.

Michael Green

⚊•⚊

There was so much blue on the scoreboard it was like a Tory landslide on election night – if you can remember that far back.

Oliver Holt on Europe's decisive victory
over America in the 2006 Ryder Cup

⚊•⚊

Ballesteros's form is up and down more often than a whore's knickers.

Oliver Hornsby

The difference between a good golf shot and a bad one is the same as the difference between a beautiful and a plain woman – a matter of millimetres.

Ian Fleming

Corey Pavin plays golf as if he were double-parked and left the meter running. Guys move slower leaving hotel fires.

Jim Murray

Asking Jack Nicklaus to re-design Augusta was like asking Andy Warhol to re-paint the Sistine Chapel.

David Feherty

He took a swing like a man with a wasp under his shirt and his pants on fire, trying to impale a butterfly on the end of a scythe.

Paul Gallico

To say I was disappointed would be like saying Custer had a spot of bother at Little Bighorn.

Tony Jacklin after poor weather and a
heckler upset his play at St Andrews

In ancient Egypt when the pharaohs died, forceps were inserted through their nostrils to pull their brains down from their skulls. I feel roughly the same sensation when I watch golf.

Kevin Myers

PLAYING IT BY
THE BOOK

The only proper use
for a golf book is to
balance it on your
head so you can keep
still during the swing.

Michael McDonnell

I read a strange book on golf
the other day. The foreword
wasn't by Peter Alliss.

Chris Plumridge

You hit the ball onto the fairway,
you hit it onto the green, and
then you knock it into a hole. So
why, please, the 3,417 books?

Lily Tomlin

There are more books in America
on how to hit a middle-iron than
there are on thoracic surgery since
doctors stopped working out of
the back rooms of barber shops.

Peter Andrews

SANDBAGGERS

Lawrence of Arabia, Tarbuck of Las Brisas... when you speak of sand, we have been there.

Jimmy Tarbuck

At my age it's tough trying
to get out of the bunkers. I
mean *after* I've hit the ball.

George Burns

A sand trap is a deep depression
of sand, filled with golfers
in deep depressions.

Henry Beard

Johnny Miller gets balls out of the
bunker as smoothly as a man lifting
a breast out of an evening gown.

Phil Harris

A poor golfer sent his ball into a bunker. 'What club should I use?' he asked his caddy in some desperation. 'Don't worry about the club,' the caddy replied, 'just bring plenty of food and water.'

Robert Powell

I once took 12 shots to get out of a bunker in Surrey. I'm told the Hamlet cigar ad was inspired by my performance.

Tim Brooke-Taylor

If your adversary is badly bunkered, there's no rule against your standing over him and counting his strokes aloud with increasing gusto as their number mounts up.

Horace Hutchinson

PUTTERING OUT

You can take a man's wife. You can even take his wallet. But never on any account take his putter.

Archie Compston

The less said about the putter
the better. It is an instrument of
torture, designed by Tantalus and
forged in the devil's own smithy.

Tony Lema

One-shot putters are in
better physical condition
than Paul Gascoigne.

Linford Christie

In my house in Houston I still
have the putter with which I
missed that 2 ½ foot putt to win
the Open. It's in two pieces.

Doug Sanders

When you're putting well you're a
good putter. When your opponent
is putting well he *has* a good putter.

John D. Sheridan

Tommy Bolt's putters spent more
time in the air than Lindberg.

Jimmy Demaret on the temperamental American

Do that again and you'll
wear my putter.

Bob Shearer to a photographer who distracted
him while playing a shot in 1975

Lee Trevino's patter is
better than his putter.

Nick Lundberg

PUTTERING OUT

My putter worked so well for
me today I'm going to sleep
with it tonight. My husband
will have to go next door.

Joanne Carner

◆

When you're putting well you can't
hear anything off the green. but
when you're putting badly you
can hear a man jingle two coins
in his pocket 100 yards away.

Tony Jacklin

◆

I find it helpful to inform an opponent
who's lining up a four-foot putt that
under the metric system widely used
in other countries, it's actually a
putt of just over 1,200 millimetres.

Leslie Nielsen

WATCH YOUR LANGUAGE

Golf is the easiest
game in the world to
play. You just hit the
ball and then swear.

Sid Caesar

I don't like people asking me if I golf. Using 'golf' as a verb is a bit like using sex as one. Would you say to somebody, 'Do you sex?'

David Owen

The finest golfers are the least loquacious.

P. G. Wodehouse

No problem, Greg. You don't need to talk. Just listen.

Lee Trevino to an exasperated Greg Norman who said to him, 'Do you mind if we don't talk during the game today?'

Conversation interferes with most people's golf. With Lee Trevino, golf interferes with his conversations.

Retief Goosen

———◆———

Until I actually heard it, I would not have thought it possible to speak the words, 'Just pop that one in, old boy' with such cunning inflexion that it conveyed the message, 'Please, God, help me keep a straight face when he twitches this one past the hole.'

Peter Dobereiner

———◆———

A Shi'ite effort.

David Feherty on a poor shot he played in the Dubai Desert Classic

Sean doesn't enjoy his golf as
much since he had his operation.
He can't swear as much.

Sean Connery's wife after he had laser
surgery on his throat in 1992

I don't know why people say
Ben Hogan is untalkative. He
speaks to me on every green.
He says, 'You're away.'

Jimmy Demaret

It is embarrassing for me to
play on the US circuit. I once
asked my caddy for a sand
wedge and he came back ten
minutes later with ham on rye.

Chi Chi Rodriguez

THE EGOS HAVE LANDED

I always ask my caddy to tell me two things: the yardage, and that I'm the best in the world.

Jack Nicklaus

If I can hit it I can hole it.

Arnold Palmer

Arnold Palmer doesn't so much
walk onto the first tee as climb
into it, almost as though it was a
prize ring. Then he looks round
at the gallery as though he's
trying to count the house.

Charles Price

If I didn't sign autographs
while I was walking, I'd never
make my tee-off time.

Colin Montgomerie

In my entire career I've never gone round a course like that. I never mishit a shot. Every drive was perfect, and every iron. I was in awe of myself.

Greg Norman after winning the British Open in 1993

Any time I get ideas above my station my wife says, 'Put the garbage out'.

Sandy Lyle

WHAT'S YOUR HANDICAP?

I'm a one-eyed
Jewish Negro.

Sammy Davis Jr on being asked
what his handicap was

My caddy.

Walter Travis after being asked the same question

Handicaps are allocations of strokes that permit players of very different ability to do equally poorly on the same golf course.

Henry Beard

Like all 24-handicap men, Fisher had the most perfect confidence in his ability to beat all other 24-handicap men.

P. G. Wodehouse

'What is your handicap?'
Lady Cunard asked Lord
Castlerose on the golf course.
'Drink and debauchery,' he
answered sadly but truthfully.

Philip Ziegler

—◆—

The great thing about the handicap
is that a guy who can't break 100 can
kick the shit out of Phil Mickelson.

John Daly

—◆—

I always play golf with a
handy cap on my head.

Les Dawson

171

LET'S GO CLUBBING

Most new sets of
golf clubs still include
three-irons, even
though most regular
golfers would get
more use from a
second umbrella.

David Owen

I once gave a lesson about clubs. After it was over, a lady informed me she knew how to recognise a six-iron: there were six holes in the top of the grip.

Mel Flanagan

Buddy Hackett and Jimmy Durante were once playing golf and Durante was having a particularly bad game, his score well over 200. At the end he asked Hackett what he should give his caddy. 'Your clubs,' Hackett replied.

Des Lynam

The trouble about getting a new set
of clubs is that if you're still playing
crap you have nothing to blame it on.

Ben Elton

The most exquisitely satisfying act in the world of golf is that of throwing a club. The full backswing, the delayed wrist action, the flowing follow-through, followed by that unique whirring sound, reminiscent only of a passing flock of starlings, are without parallel in sport.

Harry Longhurst

COURSES FROM HELL

There's nothing
wrong with St
Andrews that
100 bulldozers
couldn't put right.

Ed Furgol

The 13th at St Andrews is a great hole. It gives you a million options, not one of them worth a damn.

Tom Kite

Visiting St Andrews is like visiting your old grandmother. She's crotchety and eccentric but also elegant, and anyone who doesn't fall in love with her has no imagination.

Nick Faldo

When the wind blows at St Andrews, even the seagulls walk.

Nick Faldo

In the rough at Muirfield not only could you lose your golf ball, but if you left your golf bag down you could lose that too. You could even lose a short caddy.

Jack Nicklaus

If you're standing on the first tee at Sotogrande and you can see Gibraltar, rain is on the way. If you can't, it's already pissing down.

Eric Sykes

I saw Edmund Hillary at Sawgrass – and he was having a hard time keeping his balance.

Tom Weiskopf

Columbus went round the world
in 1492. That's pretty good
considering the size of the course.

Milton Berle

More players have fantasised
about killing me than they have
about killing Jack the Ripper.

Course designer Robert Trent Jones, who
was renowned for his 'sadistic' courses

Peter Dye used so much
wood, his courses may be the
first ever to burn down.

Barry McDermott on the famous architect

Golf is a cruel game anyway, so why should I design courses fairly?

Peter Dye

A golf course is comprised of 18 holes, 17 of them unnecessary, but included simply to create the maximum amount of frustration.

Terry Wogan

All Hazeltine needs is 80 acres and some cows.

Dave Hill

LET'S GET PHYSICAL

I wish it had bitten me
a little lower down.

David Feherty, whose arm swelled up to twice its
normal size after being bitten by a snake at Wentworth

My wife gave me ten oysters
last night to rouse my passion,
but only nine of them worked.

Lee Trevino

A true pro always prefers his
golf course to his intercourse.

Conan O'Brien

Would you say a golfer is a
man who putts it about?

Ben Elton

Five things that sound
dirty in golf but aren't:
1. My shaft is bent.
2. You really whacked the
hell out of that sucker.
3. Keep your head down and
spread your legs a bit more.
4. Nice stroke, but watch
your follow-through.
5. Hold on, I need to wash my balls.

Anon

A golfer is stranded on a desert island when suddenly this busty blonde arrives on a little boat. She asks him if he'd like a cigarette and he delightedly says yes, whereupon she pulls a packet out of her bra. She then asks him if he'd like a nip of whiskey. Again he says yes and again she reaches into her bra for the bottle. The pair of them lie down on the sand and she loosens her bra-straps and says, 'Would you like to play around?' The mesmerised golfer jumps up and says, 'Don't tell me you've got a set of clubs in there as well!'

Bill Kelly

Golf groupies must be the most passive of any competitive game. Even chess fans display greater vivacity.

Robert O'Byrne

COACH TRIPS

Those who can, do.
Those who can't,
teach. And those who
can't teach, teach golf.

Woody Allen

There's no element of golf
that can't be made even more
infuriating with a little coaching.

Noël Coward

Contrary to popular belief, it's
not true that golf can't be taught.
It can. But it can't be learned.

Leslie Nielsen

A good golfer doesn't need a
coach. All he needs is a cart.

Peter Lawford

ALLISS IN BLUNDERLAND

The strange phrases of Peter Alliss

You could see
Parnevik's heart
visibly drop.

Bernhard Langer is considered
a good putter from this range,
irrespective of his reputation.

Y ou couldn't find two more
completely different personalities
than these two men, Tom
Watson and Brian Barnes.
One is the complete golf
professional and the other the
complete professional golfer.

He used to be fairly indecisive,
but now he's not so sure.
And now to hole eight, which
is, in fact, the 8th hole.

THE ICONS

Nick Faldo's idea
of excitement is
having his After
Eight mints at 7.30.

Graham Elliott

I've had a bad week. But in
the real world a bad week is
waking up and finding you're a
steelworker in Scunthorpe.

Nick Faldo

Jack Nicklaus is a legend
in his spare time.

Tom Watson

They keep talking about the Big
Four – Palmer, Nicklaus, Player and
Trevino. I just want to be the fifth
wheel in case somebody gets a flat.

Chi Chi Rodriguez

I don't have an image or a nickname.
Maybe I should dye my hair
peroxide blonde and call myself
The Great White Tadpole.

Ian Woosnam

❈

Walter Hagen said he came out to
play a match once carrying a fifth of
whiskey and still wearing a tux from
the night before, but I'll bet he went
to bed at ten o'clock, got up at six to
put the tux on, then went outside and
fell in three bushes to get it dirty.

Lee Trevino on Hagen's playboy image

❈

Arnold Palmer would go for the flag
from the middle of an alligator's back.

Lee Trevino

Golf was a comparatively sexless enterprise before Arnold Palmer came along. His caveman approach took audiences by storm. He was Cagney pushing a grapefruit in Mae Clark's face, Gable kicking the door down to Scarlett O'Hara's bedroom.

Jim Murray

Sam Snead has a terrific pair of legs. He's double-jointed. He can stand flat-footed in a room and kick an eight-foot ceiling.

Lee Trevino

John Daly could draw a crowd in Saskatchewan.

Rocco Mediate

Seve Ballesteros hits
the ball farther than
I go on my holidays.

Lee Trevino

Tiger Woods has such a lazy style, last week I caught him nodding off on his backswing.

Valerie Netter

Tiger Woods is super-rich, super-successful and married to a beautiful woman, yet he rarely smiles. One wonders how he'd look if he was a poor loser married to a dog.

Steve Jeffares

Knock knock.
Who's there?
Tiger.
Tiger who?
Ah, the fickleness of fame.

Anon

Tiger Woods may well be an android from an alien planet who landed here in a spacecraft and who occasionally loses tournaments on purpose so people won't suspect.

Martin Johnson

PERENNIAL LAWS
OF THE GAME

A golf ball will always
travel furthest when hit
in the wrong direction.

Henry Beard

Most good shots are accidents.

Eugene Black

He who swisheth most, driveth least.

Michael Green

Every golfer knows that a
ball only bounces off a tree
in the direction of the hole if
there's a bunker in the way.

Sid Caesar

The number of tees in your bag is always less than 3 or more than 600.

Michael Ryan

—◆—

Golf gifts given to us by non-golfers are invariably useless.

Sergio Garcia

—◆—

Golf is all about preparation. First you get your clubs, then you rehearse your excuses, then you play.

Phil Silvers

SENIOR CITIZENS

I know exactly when
I want to retire now,
but when I reach
that time I may not.

Jack Nicklaus

People ask me why I still play golf
at my age. I have to. I'm too old for
marbles and too married for women.

Bob Hope

—◆—

We don't stop playing because
we get old. We get old
because we stop playing.

Walter Hagen

—◆—

One of the nice things about the
seniors tour is that we can take a
cart and a cooler. If your game isn't
going well, you can have a picnic.

Lee Trevino

Men chase golf balls
when they're too old
to chase anything else.

Groucho Marx

BYE BYE BIRDIE

My boss told me
I needed to de-
stress myself so he
suggested golf. It was
a very wise suggestion.
I gave it up.

Ben Cabot

He enjoys that perfect peace,
that peace beyond all human
understanding, that peace which
cometh at its maximum only to
a man who has given up golf.

P. G. Wodehouse

———•———

I'm fed up of reading about retired
tennis players taking up golf. When
I retire, I'm going to take up tennis.

Jimmy Demaret

———•———

I gave up golf for painting because
it takes me less strokes.

Dwight D. Eisenhower

When I retire I'm going to get a
pair of grey slacks, a white shirt, a
striped tie, a blue blazer and a case
of dandruff and go stand on the first
tee so I can be a USGA official.

Lee Trevino

It's time to give up golf when
birds flying south readjust their
flight patterns to let you hit.

Richard Miziner

That was a great game
of golf, fellers.

Bing Crosby's reputed last words

THE LAST LAUGH

A golfer was taking so much care before driving from the 5th tee that his partner asked, 'Why the concentration?' 'I'm very anxious to make this shot a good one,' said his partner. 'My mother-in-law is down there in the clubhouse watching me.'

'Impossible,' said his mate. 'You could never hit her at that distance.'

George Coote

While the ethics of golf forbid coughing, talking, sneering, snoring or making any other sort of noise while our opponent addresses the ball, it is not illegal to throw flares or tickle his ears with a wisp of straw.

Ring Lardner

He seemed to be attempting to deceive his ball and lull it into a false sense of security by looking away from it and then making a lightning slash in the apparent hope of catching it off its guard.

P. G. Wodehouse

Aubrey Malone has compiled a number of quotation anthologies and humour books, as well as books on films, celebrities and famous writers.

www.summersdale.com